good grief?

sharing a personal journey

good grief?

© Jacqui and Andrew Parkinson 2012

Written and produced by Jacqui and Andrew Parkinson

Artwork © Jacqui Parkinson
Photography © Andrew Parkinson

First published 2012.

ISBN 978-0-9571518-0-2

A catalogue record of this book is available from the British Library.

Published by
THREADS PUBLISHING
Higher Lawn, Chudleigh, Newton Abbot, Devon TQ13 0LF

www.threadspublishing.co.uk

designed by Barrie Cutler, Gomango Creative, Chudleigh, Devon TQ13 0HX
printed by Short Run Press, Exeter EX2 7LW

Introductions

This book creatively, simply and uniquely expresses the pain that tears apart the bereaved — yet it just as simply describes the healing process. I think it's a lovely gift to help someone smile and also feel free to weep.

When someone you know suffers a bereavement, it's very hard to know what to do. It's hard enough for them to concentrate on anything in the first couple of years, and they can feel totally distant from books and articles. Reading material for the bereaved is often written by people who are either almost recovered, or by experts who look at grief rather academically. When you've just lost a partner, you're at the start of a journey, but writers can seem to you as though they're far down the journey - and far from you.

Jacqui's book is very different. It comes from the hard personal experience of one very recently bereaved widow. It is extraordinarily original, expressive and incisive.

Jacqui is a very skilled textile artist, but she doesn't use her skills to promote herself. She uses them to touch people, to move them, to surprise them. It's a human and spiritual connexion that's at the heart of her work. And at the heart of this book are feelings shared by so many men and women gripped by sorrow.

Fiona Castle, OBE

Two of the most difficult things about grief is that it can isolate us and silence us. If you are bereaved, you can feel that there is no one else feeling as you do. You keep so many of your thoughts unspoken. You tell yourself off for being weak or silly. And if you're on the other side, trying to support a bereaved person, you sense their isolation but feel helpless or embarrassed about how to reach out. You probably try to make things 'normal'. Perhaps you encourage someone saying that they're doing really well - which often simply means they're not crying!

So often, conversations skirt around the vital things of life after a death. In this book, Jacqui addresses the real issues. It's frighteningly honest, even provocative, but above all filled with the most amazing hope.

Rob Parsons, OBE, Founder and Chairman, Care for the Family

Jacqui's journey: - stitching through the tears

My first husband, Rob Frost, was a Methodist minister. As a minister's wife I was no stranger to death and funerals. I was used to trying to console people in sadness and grief.

But I wasn't prepared for the knock-out blow of grief when Rob died of cancer in 2007.

Like so many bereaved people, I felt wounded physically and emotionally. It seemed that I'd lost my identity and all sense of direction in my life. What's more, personal circumstances forced me to move, out of London from my home of more than twenty years, to Devon. While Rob and I had spent many holidays there, I knew hardly anyone, and my sense of isolation was acute. People I met in the community were friendly enough but didn't know how to deal with this widowed stranger.

from sorrow to stitching

It was a bleak, very lonely time. I had some work as a textile artist, but felt an additional need to link my grief with some artistic and also physical actions. So I took up running, partly to obliterate my thoughts and partly to try to feel energised about something. I'd never run before, and certainly never saw myself as a runner - the idea and practice literally took my breath away!

As I ran, often totally blank in my mind, suddenly I'd start sobbing for no apparent reason. Then words from the pit of my stomach would churn up into my mind.

Words and phrases came into my head when I was running or sat exhausted on a bench where Rob and I used to sit together. First I would remember fragments and scribble them down when I got home. Later I'd take pen and paper with me. I didn't rewrite them, but I shared them with a close friend who made a few edits.

Slowly I also started to develop ideas of how these words might form a part of some artwork that could be an outlet for my feelings.

The previous year, for no particular reason, I had started to collect antique handkerchiefs.

I wondered: could I use them as a canvas for my grief?

Why vintage handkerchiefs? Working on them felt particularly appropriate, because I always had the sense of sharing my grieving with other people from earlier generations. There I was, working by myself, and yet not alone.

Whose tears, I wondered, had fallen into these women's hankies? Maybe someone like me had mourned the loss of her husband? Had someone wept for a son lost in a war? Did the sadness for a still-born child stain the cloth of these hankies? Had a girl cried into this hanky when her mother died?

The action of stitching through the tears was calming and made me feel much less isolated. The repetitive action of pulling threads through fabric, the focus on tiny details, intricate beading, couched threads - so many small elements playing a part in a larger picture all helped my sometimes wildly disordered thoughts.

And, just like crying, you know you are sharing the actions of stitching with people who have gone on before you.

So I started stitching on the hankies, building up a set of very varied pieces. It was entirely personal and private. And it was all relatively unplanned, never carefully worked out designs … a ritual of running, writing, stitching and grieving.

I didn't plan, I just stitched, worked intuitively, kept going through the turmoil of my thoughts and fears. I followed my feelings, for example picking up a dark stone here or a red bead there, sewing them on as my mood took me. I had some of the hankies printed with photographs of a remembered landscape or an important image. I'd think of odd phrases which resonated with my loneliness, and I'd recall words from the Bible which reflected my sadness. Songs came through my head, some of which I stitched.

My experience is that the physical activities - from stitching to running - can free up the mind wonderfully, and really allow the brain to abseil!

So I ended up in 2007 with a set of fifteen handkerchiefs, a record of my personal journey, ready to be packed away out of sight. Not polished pieces an artist would like to display, but the raw ramblings of my grief.

from hankies to cathedrals

I didn't originally intend the handkerchiefs to be for public display, as they seemed to me to be so personal. But friends convinced me that they have a universal quality which could - and now does - touch a wider audience. It was a strange paradox: I am used to seeing my work on display and some of my thoughts, but not my innermost feelings!

The Deo Gloria Trust who have promoted textile exhibitions in cathedrals kindly backed me in this venture, so from the hankies came the exhibition "good grief?" which started touring cathedrals in England in 2010.

My sadness was shared. Here, on display, are words (my words) - images (my images) - and ideas (my ideas) - which resonate with many widows and widowers, and also may touch anyone who has been bereaved. 'My' ideas, 'my' words, 'my' images encompass things which so many people have cried about, and will continue to cry over, into their own handkerchiefs. 'My' issues of identity, loss, personality and faith in darkest times, given a public airing in the exhibition, prove to be 'theirs', 'yours' and 'ours': mine alone, and yet also shared by millions.

from exhibition to book

Many viewers have been very moved by the exhibition, and many seem to find that in some way it gives them a voice for their grief. And now from the exhibition developed the idea of a book, triggered by very touching and encouraging words made by visitors to the cathedrals in conversations and comments books.

What kind of book, though? Graphic, not wordy; raw and direct, something that carries my emotions and other people's in our different journeys. I wanted something really personal and yet easily identifiable, something that meets grief head on for me - and you.

Two years later, I suddenly felt able to face the task. I made a series of linocut prints, stark black and white images both reflecting my feelings now and recalling past feelings. I made a very tatty doll which showed what I felt I was like: no features, no expression, wired inside and able to take up all kinds of contorted poses. I wanted to express my grief - our grief - still reaching out for help or sympathy or encouragement. The doll was very important for me because it just showed how I felt with its arms extended, reaching out to other people and to God, or crouched in a corner or curled round cocooning myself from the outside world.

I used hand lettering and cut out paper letters to make it a real person's writing and not neat tidy computer-generated text.

Producing this book helped me to distance myself from my painful situation, from Rob's death and my loneliness and sadness. Expressing myself through the hankies and then the book meant there were physical objects which put my grief in a time and place. And allowed me to begin to discover some distance.

from me to you

You have in your hand something that's not so much a polished product, but more an output of raw materials! It is the working out of one person's feelings, part of one person's journey – mine, during very difficult times. And as with many raw materials, you may want to pick and choose, make use of the bits you like and leave the bits you don't find so useful.

What I hope is that these pages may provide some - maybe only small - encouragement in dark times. Perhaps they will reduce someone's isolation - maybe yours - just a bit, maybe in some of the loneliest moments. I hope they will help people's tears - maybe yours - ebb and flow too, as they did mine, as you join my journey briefly, and carry on your own.

ALL MY MEMORIES begin WITH (WE)

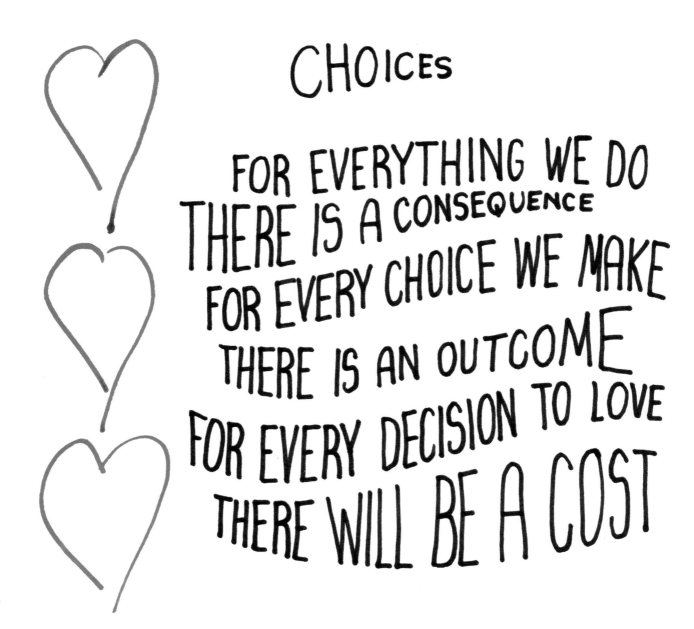

CHOICES

FOR EVERYTHING WE DO
THERE IS A CONSEQUENCE
FOR EVERY CHOICE WE MAKE
THERE IS AN OUTCOME
FOR EVERY DECISION TO LOVE
THERE WILL BE A COST

none of us knows how
to do
grief

we stumble on
falling over
getting up
trying
to make sense of isolated lives somehow
pain beyond understanding
loneliness that overwhelms
none of us knows how
to do .
grief

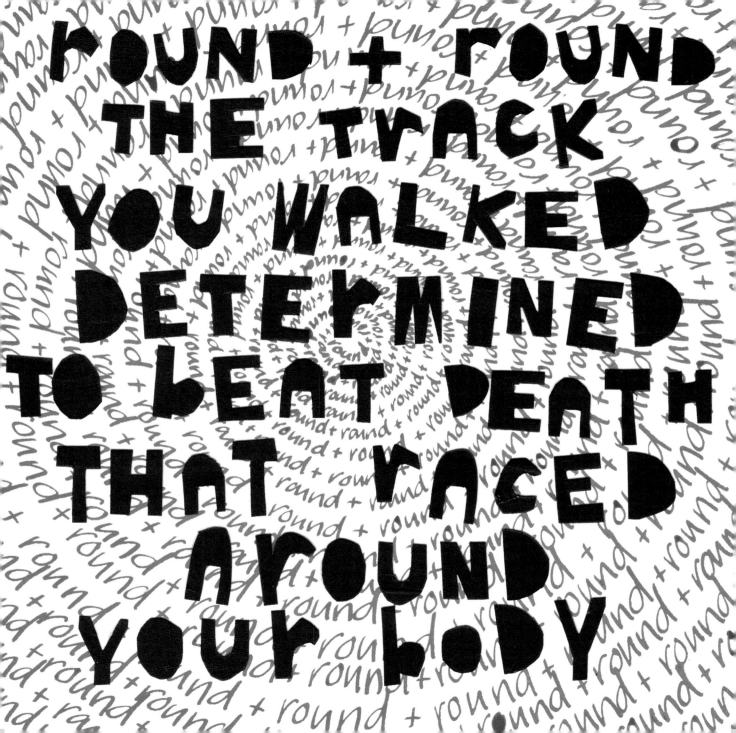

round + round the track you walked determined to beat death that raced around your body

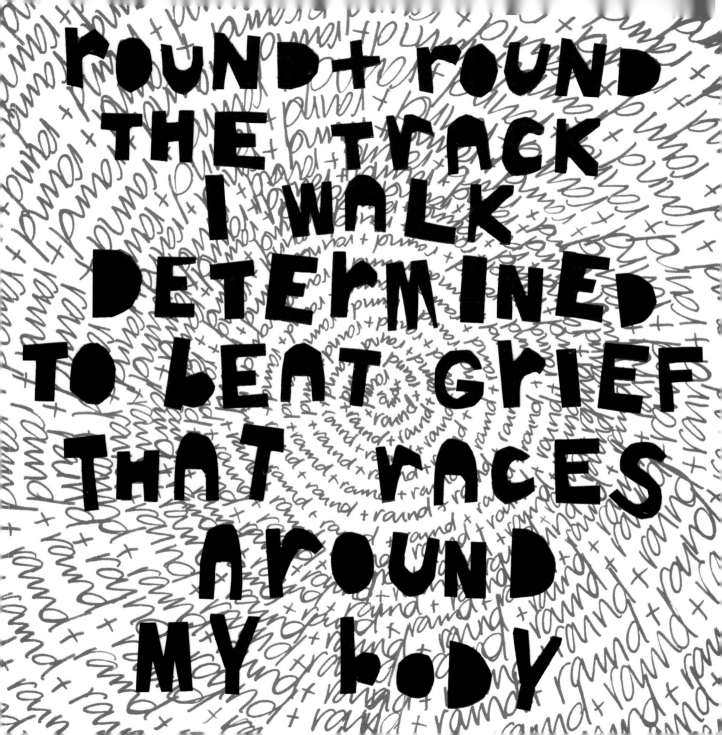

ROUND + ROUND
THE TRACK
I WALK
DETERMINED
TO BEAT GRIEF
THAT RACES
AROUND
MY BODY

WHY? cancercancercancercancercancercancer
cancercancercancercancercancer
cancercancercancercancer
cancercancercancercancer
cancercancercancer
cancercancercancer
cancer
THE RAIN FALLS
ON THE GOOD + BAD
ALIKE

LONG REACH OF CANCER
cancercancer
cancercancercancer
THE BIG
cancer
cancercancer
cancercancercancer
cancercancercancer
cancercancer
cancercancer
cancercancercancer
cancercancercancer

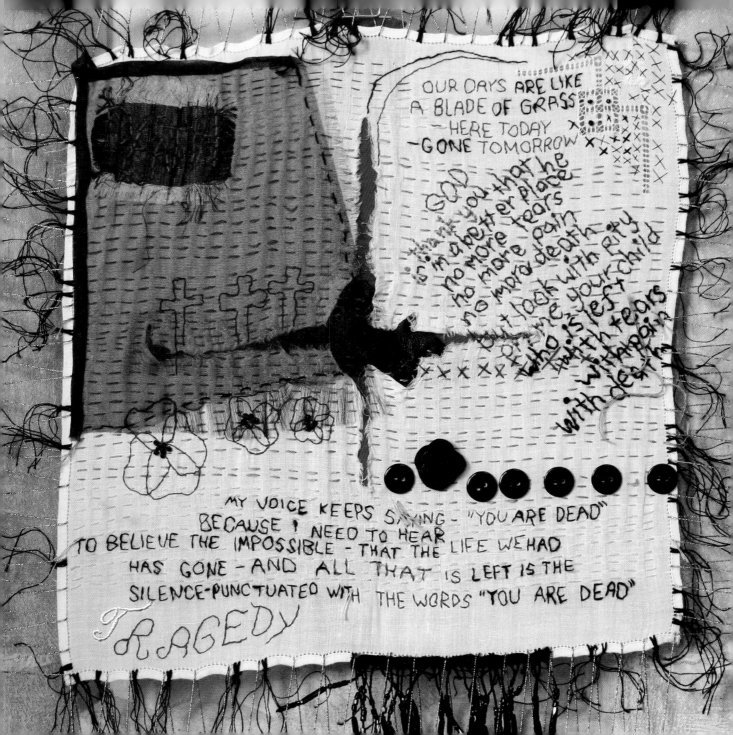

BINGO

GAME WON AND LOST

WHO LOST
YOU OR ME
IS DEATH THE PRIZE OF A LIFE WELL LIVED
AND LIFE THE COST PAID BY THOSE LEFT BEHIND
OR IS DEATH THE CUTTING SHORT OF DREAMS
AND LIFE THE HOPE THAT THERE IS MORE

WHO LOST
WHO WON
GAME WON AND LOST
BINGO

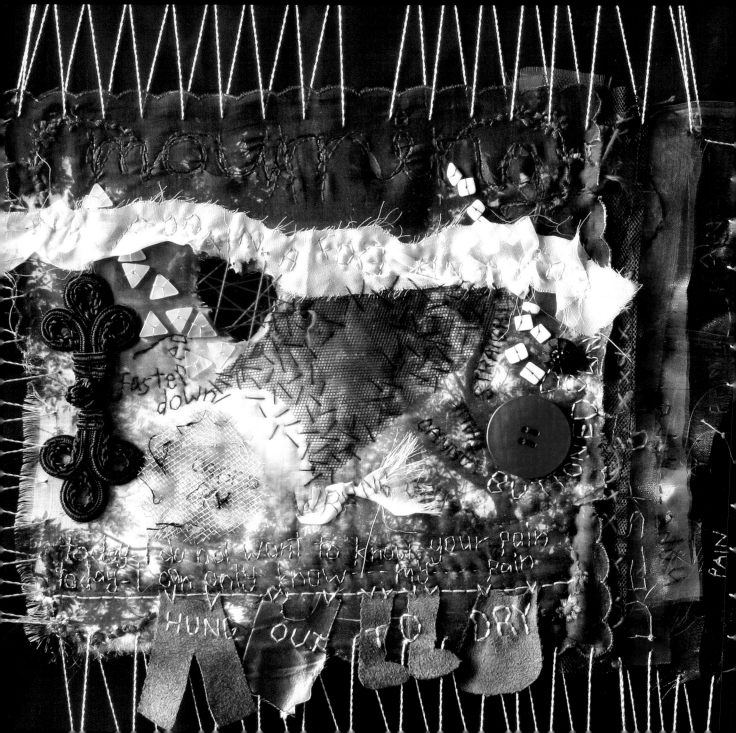

TOO MUCH INFORMATION

TODAY
I DO NOT WANT TO KNOW
YOUR PAIN
YOUR GRIEF
YOUR LOSS

TODAY
I CAN ONLY KNOW
MY PAIN
MY GRIEF
MY LOSS

DEATH
IS NOT APPROPRIATE
IN ANY SITUATION
FOR ANY BODY

UNDER ANY CIRCUMSTANCE

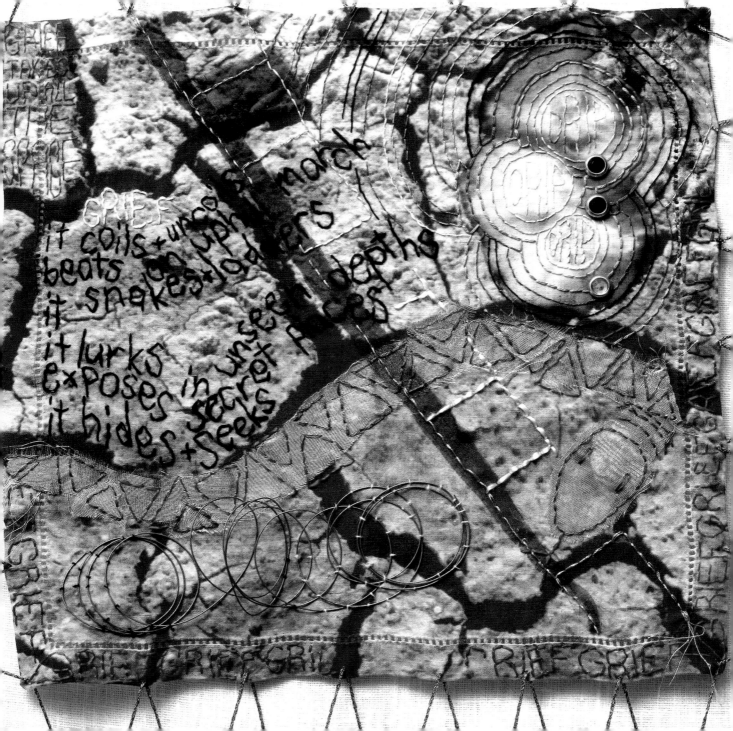

he WILL noT
come back
he WILL never
come back
he is noT
coMinG back
he is dead

tears
tears for you flow again
unbidden
from some deep reservoir of water
submerged hidden secret
deep in the depths of my soul they flood
no damned words to stop their escape
released for all to see
reservoirs to bring refreshment
cleansing life

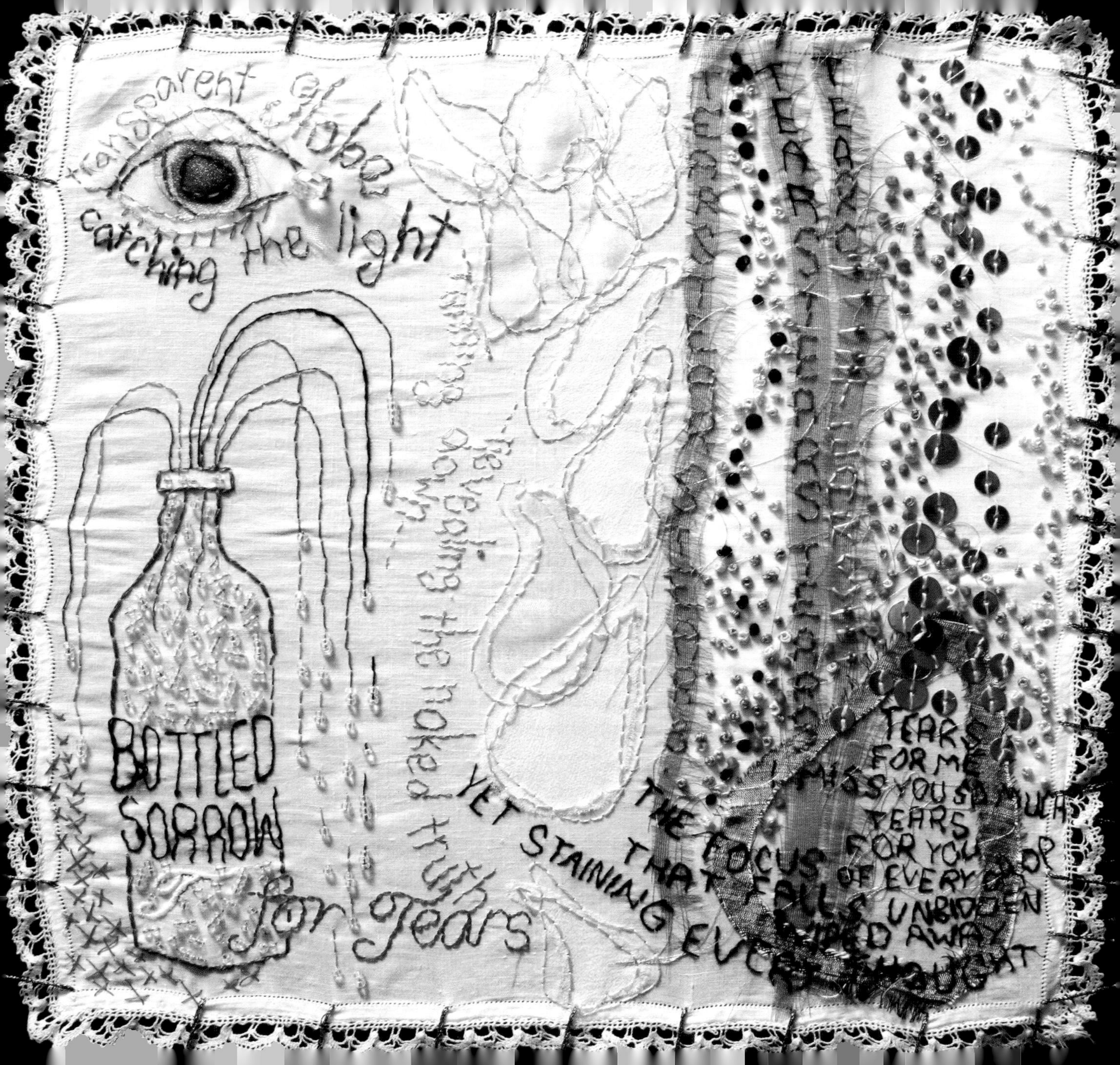

transparent globe
catching the light

BOTTLED
SORROW
for tears

revealing the naked truth

YET STAINING EVERY
THAT FALLS

TEARS
FOR ME
IT HAS YOU SO MUCH
TEARS
FOR YOU OF
THE FOCUS OF EVERY DROP
THAT FALLS UNBIDDEN
WIPED AWAY
EVERY THOUGHT

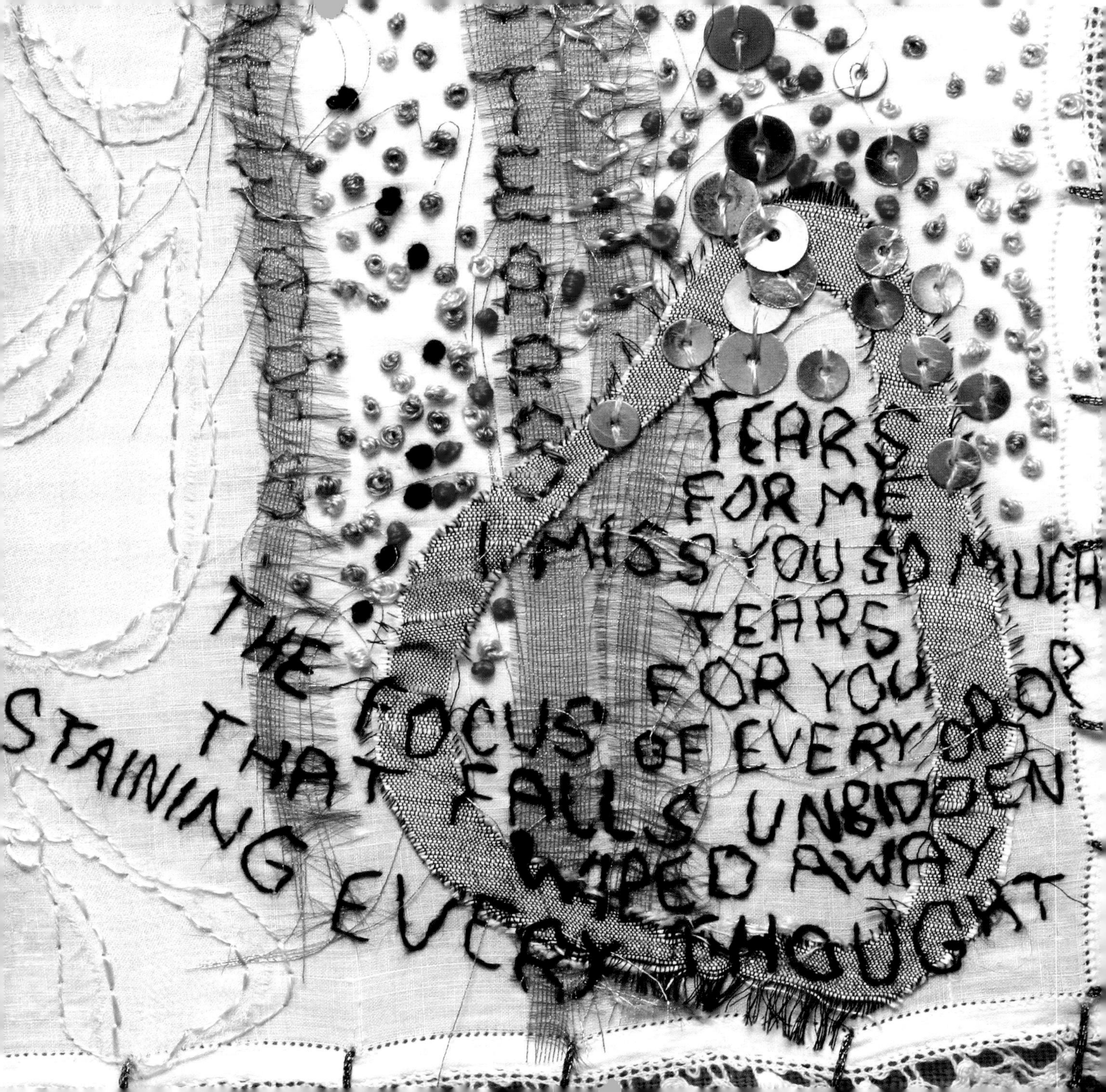

TEARS
FOR ME
I MISS YOU SO MUCH
TEARS
FOR YOU
THE FOCUS OF EVERY DROP
THAT FALLS UNBIDDEN
STAINING WIPED AWAY
EVERY THOUGHT

I KNOW I AM
one In a MILLIon WHO
GrIeves THIs day
and THere are MANY
WHo suffer More
THan I can IMaGIne
but yeT
I can noT— WILL noT
suffocaTe THe GrIeF
I Have InsIde

NO SKIN ON SKIN
NO SKIN ON SKIN
NO INTIMACY
NO INTIMACY

NO SPOONING
NO SPOONING

MISSING
FROM MY SIDE
FROM MY BED
FROM MY ARMS
MISSING
YET FOUND IN EVERY THOUGHT
SQUEEZED INTO ALL ACTIVITY
ALWAYS PRESENT
MISSING
PRESUMED DEAD

NIGHT TIME

55 · 56 · 57 · 58 · 59 · 60 · 64 · 69 · 79

11 · 12 · 13 · 14 · 15 · 16 · 17 · 18 · 19 · 20 · 21 · 22 · 23 · 24 · 25 · 26 · 27 · 28 · 29 · 30 · 31 · 32 · 33 · 34 · 35

I Lie
alone in a bed
made
for two
alone in a bed
I think
you will return
I Lie

GOOD?
NIGHT

I have moved
to the centre
of the bed
neither my side
nor your side
but the space between
the inbetween space

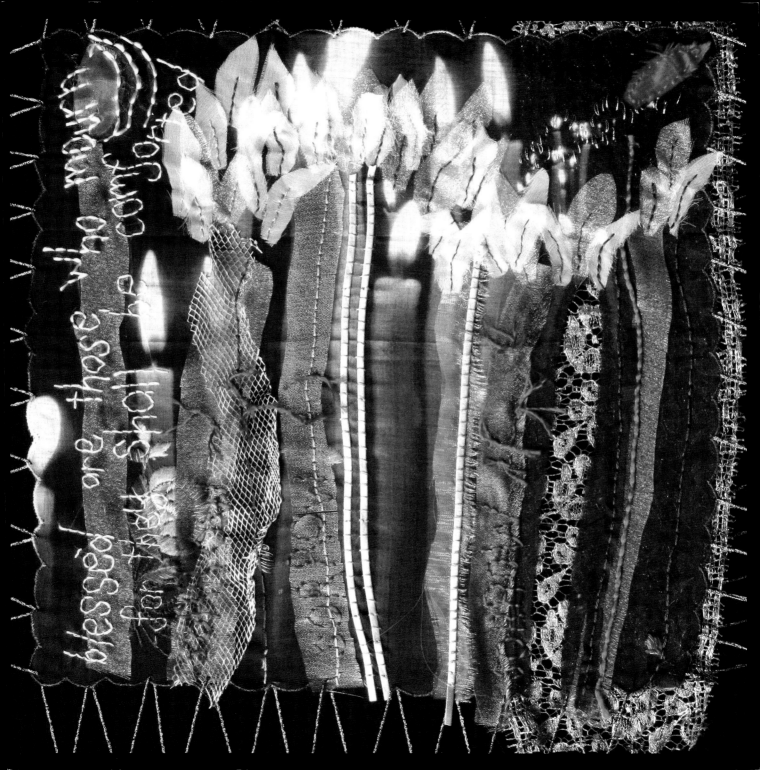

blessed are those who mourn, for they shall be comforted

time in time in time in time in time in time

I COULD NOT IMAGINE
A TIME
WHEN
I WOULD NOT TALK
CONSTANTLY
ABOUT YOUR DAY
BUT - IT CAME

I COULD NOT IMAGINE
A TIME
WHEN
I DO NOT TALK
CONSTANTLY
ABOUT YOUR LIFE
BUT - IT WILL COME

PAST PRESENT FUTURE

Summer --- Spring --- Winter --- Autumn

SEP-OCT-NOV-DEC

MINUTES→HOURS→DAYS→YEARS→DECADES

SUN-MON-TUE-WED-THURS-FRI-SAT

THOUGHTS OF AGEING ALONE
INTO THE YEARS AHEAD
SO STRANGE
UNBELIEVABLE

A BORDERLESS PAGE
WITH NO WORDS
A STIFF CANVAS
WITH NO PAINT
A STRETCH OF FABRIC
WITH NO STITCH

SO HOW TO BEGIN
THE YEARS AHEAD
ALONE

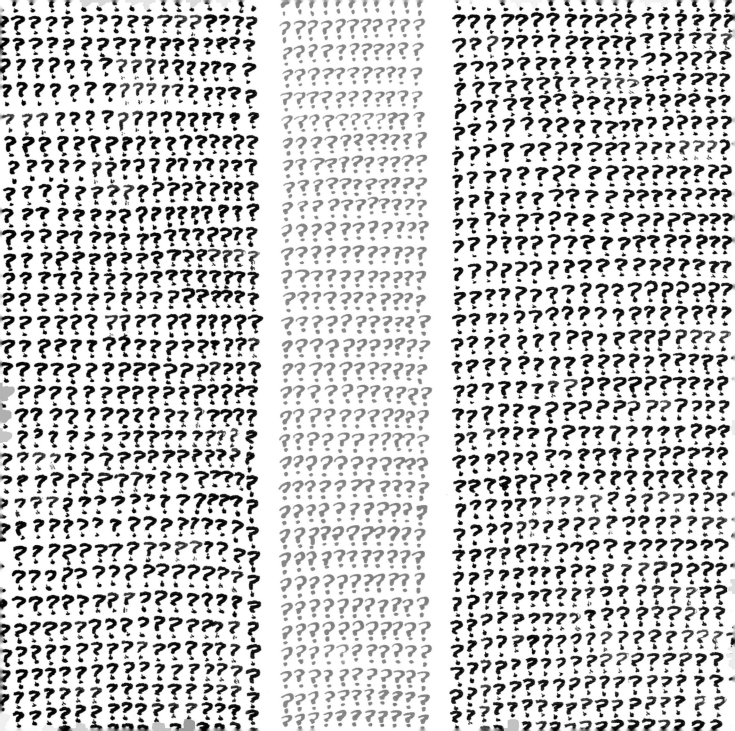

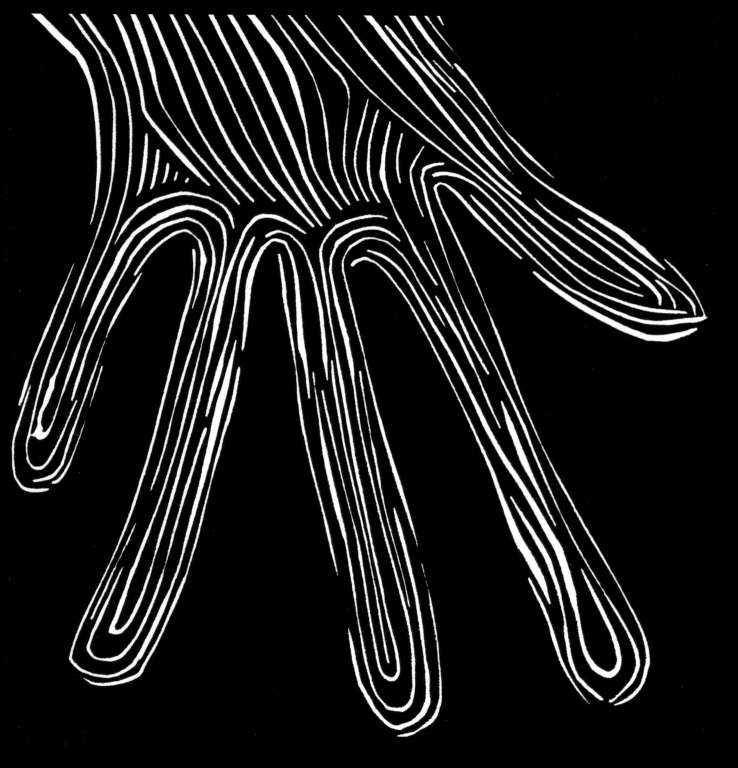

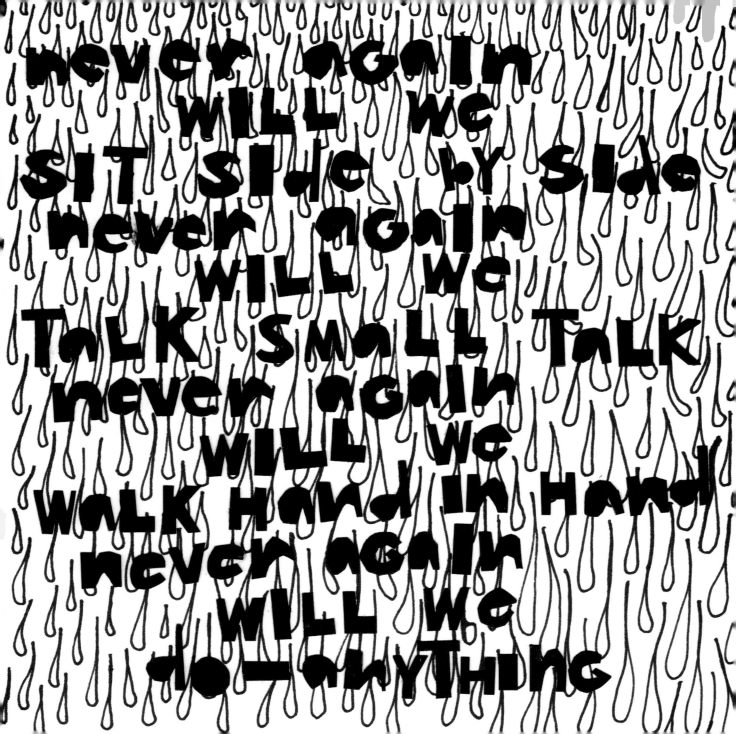

REDEEM
THE PAIN - THE AGONY - THE DEATH
DO THE IMPOSSIBLE

THE INVISIBLE
IN THE ORDINARY AGONY
OF THE EVERY DAY
MAKING NEW
HEALING - CLEANSING - RESTORING

REDEEMING LORD

THANK YOU
FOR GIVING ME A VOICE
TO SPEAK THE WORDS
WHICH ARE NOT
SPEAKABLE
TO SAY THE THINGS
WHICH ARE NOT
SAYABLE
TO SHOUT THE
OBSCENITY
WHICH IS DEATH

AS YOU SLIP AWAY
INTO THE PAST
I STRUGGLE
TO LET YOU GO
TO ACCEPT THAT
THIS IS LIFE NOW
WITHOUT YOU

future future

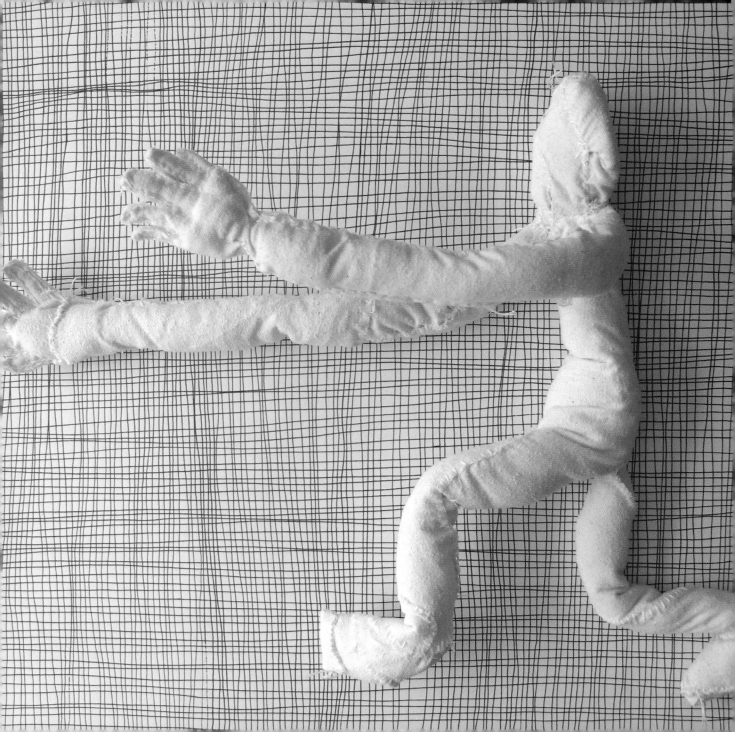

The Man
Plucks The banjo
and There is Music

The Music
Plucks My heart
and There are Tears

troubles melt like lemon drops
Away above the chimney pots
That's where you'll find me

SOMEWHERE OVER THE RAINBOW

on keeping on

YOUR GOD-CREATED IDENTITY LIVE GENEROUSLY

someday I'll wish upon a star
And wake up when the clouds are
far behind me
troubles melt like lemon drops
Away above the chimney pots
that's where you'll find me

HERE OVER THE RAINBOW

dancing
alone
grieving for past memories
dancing
alone
rejoicing for past memories

Continuing the journey

These pages aren't the end of the story, of course. Here I am on the last page, with L plates on, learning how to live some kind of new life in a new place. Geographically and emotionally, I was somewhere I wouldn't have chosen to be. But I know I do want to live my life.

At some times, grief can be so painful, so overwhelming, and everything in the world can feel wrong. People will tell you that time heals, that you'll move on, and at some times you simply can't believe them. For months - for years - it may not be true. But very slowly, as months and years pass, your life does change.

From feeling that nothing is right or normal, you start to develop your own new 'normal' existence, which doesn't hurt so much. From overcast skies, you start to see breaks in the clouds, and even appreciate the sunshine.

The grip of grief gets less - but still occasionally it can unexpectedly grab you … in a remembered place … a scribbled note … an anniversary …. a celebration of new life. Sometimes it can touch and even overwhelm you again, and this may continue from time to time for the rest of your life.

Grief can act as a block to getting on with real life. For example, sometimes you feel you are walking about with a sign round your neck saying 'widow', and you struggle with your identity in terms of Mrs - Miss - Ms … and that's all that defines you. But someone else's death should not define you, however central that person was in your life. You don't become a non-person when you become single through death.

Some people deny or smother their grief. I have found that facing it, accepting it and living with it helps me better on my personal journey. You learn that your life can take on different dimensions through sadness and joy. You don't stop grieving, you just do it less and less. Things may go grey again, but there is a life after a death, lighter and gentler than the harsh times of early grief. Even if it's not the life you would have chosen.

Is grief good? I don't know. It often hurts too much! When someone dies, life can feel entirely grey and bleak. One day, perhaps, like me, you'll find it's less heavy, and you'll start to see new colours in your life and recognise a future that's brighter – just a little bit at a time!

Further information

If you or a friend have been affected by bereavement, it may be very helpful to know about the following organisations ....

WAY Foundation

WAY aims to support young widowed men and women as they adjust to life after the death of their partner – whether that was a month, a year, or ten years ago. It was founded in 1997 and now has around 1,500 members in self-help groups across England, Scotland, Wales and Northern Ireland.

WAY's local groups provide a sympathetic environment where young widows and widowers can meet each other, socialise, make friends and offer each other support. Anyone who was widowed up to and including the age of 50 can join WAY. It doesn't matter if they are 51 or over now, but they have to have been widowed under the age of 51.

www.wayfoundation.org.uk

tel: 0300 012 4929

email: info@wayfoundation.org.uk

The WAY Foundation, Suite 35, St Loyes House, 20 St Loyes Street, Bedford, MK40 1ZL

Care for the Family

Care for the Family is a national charity which aims to promote strong family life and to help those who face family difficulties. Together with a great team of supporters and staff, it often makes a profound impact on many people's lives, helping to strengthen marriages, support parents and help bereaved people, through special events, resources, training and networks of befrienders.

www.careforthefamily.org.uk
tel: 029 2081 0800

email: mail@cff.org.uk

Care for the Family, Garth House
Leon Avenue, Cardiff, CF15 7RG

Cruse

Cruse Bereavement Care offers face-to-face and telephone support and information to anyone bereaved by death. Cruse has local branches throughout England, Wales and Northern Ireland and its services are completely free. It also provides training on bereavement care to businesses and health and social care providers.

www.cruse.org.uk Helpline: 0844 477 9400
email: helpline@cruse.org.uk

Young people's website: www.rd4u.co.uk
Young people's helpline: 0808 808 1677
Cruse Bereavement Care
PO Box 800, Richmond
Surrey, TW9 1RG

DIOCESE
OF EXETER
THE CHURCH
OF ENGLAND
IN DEVON

The Diocese of Exeter has kindly supported the publication of this book.

Central to the Gospel is the call to love one another into becoming more human. Caring relationships are key to the abundant life which God offers for all.

Much of the time we actually live in a broken and unfair world, marked by an unequal sharing of both resources and suffering. Everyday life can be fragile and we are called to support one another especially at times of vulnerability and fragmentation. For some this happens when they are excluded from the wider community because of financial or social disadvantage, for others because of the prejudicial action of others or of society itself.

For almost all of us, our vulnerability is perhaps most acute when we face issues of death, loss and grieving. Our world falls apart as a key relationship (or relationships) disappears. Losing close family and friends can leave a huge hole in our social and even spiritual fabric.

'Good grief' is a moving book, written from the experience of personal tragedy, which enables us to grow and develop new life and hope in the face of personal bereavement and pain. At the Diocese of Exeter, we are pleased to be backing this book as a means of sharing and addressing issues of loss and recovery in a unique way.

Martyn Goss, Director of Church & Society, Diocese of Exeter

ACKNOWLEDGEMENTS

I'm very grateful for the support, valuable feedback and encouragement given by countless people as I started to think about publishing this book. I would particularly like to thank the following:

Sarah Phillips for helping to edit my words and phrases and all her encouragement to publish; Martyn Goss of the Diocese of Exeter and Sue Topalian of the Diocese of Bristol for their practical support; Eric Thompson and the Deo Gloria Trust for providing the opportunity to put the handkerchiefs on view; Catherine Mackenzie and staff at Cruse for their invaluable positive criticism; Richard Baxendale, Fiona Castle, Caroline Doughty, Sonya Fisher, Sheila Fletcher, Reverend Ronald Frost, Andy and Jo Frost, Chris and Jo Frost, Celia Gaffney, Fiona Halstead, Bridget Holland, Alison Hull, Anna Jansen, Bob Kitching, Esther Langrish, Anne and Howard Liebermann, Mary Mann, Linda Palmer, Ann and Tony Parkinson, Rob Parsons, Mason and Nora Porter, Becky Totterdell, and the Trustees of New Creations, for their help, suggestions and belief in this project.

ABOUT THE ARTIST

Jacqui Parkinson was born in Manchester and lived in London for over 20 years before moving to Devon after her first husband died in 2007. She works as a textile artist specialising in artwork for display in cathedrals in England.

For details of Jacqui's exhibitions including 'good grief?', and details of 'Threads through life and faith', a book on Jacqui's cathedral displays supported by the Deo Gloria Trust, see www. cathedralexhibition. org.uk. See www.jacqui-textile.com for details of her other work.

Forthcoming publications

• A GRIEF DISPLAYED - a book showing the whole set of 'good grief?' handkerchiefs in detail.

• LIFE LOSS & LAUNDRIES - traditional and contemporary stitch resonating with the lives of Victorian laundry girls.